Soul Searching and other poems

By Pranab Ghosh

Scarlet Leaf

2017

Pranab Ghosh - Soul Searching and other poems

*Pranab Ghosh   -   Soul Searching
and other poems*

SCARLET LEAF PUBLISHING HOUSE

TORONTO ONTARIO CANADA

COPYRIGHT BY PRANAB GHOSH

ISBN: 978-1-988827-44-5

All rights reserved.

No part of this book can be used or reproduced in any manner whatsoever without written permission, except in the case of brief quotations embodied in critical articles and reviews.

For information address:

Scarlet Leaf Publishing House:

scarletleafpublishinghouse@gmail.com

*Pranab Ghosh   -   Soul Searching
and other poems*

Dedication:

*To my Mother, Purnima,
Wife, Pamela and
Daughter, Rajita*

Soul Searching

You sit with your eyes closed

You feel your soul transported
beyond the void

You sit with your eyes closed

You feel your soul touching your

super conscious self.

You sit with your eyes closed

Your soul searches your life within.

You sit with your eyes closed

Your soul touches your life within.

Pranab Ghosh   -   Soul Searching
and other poems

You sit with your eyes closed

You feel in unison with your soul.

You sit with your eyes closed

Eternal light engulfs

your soul, your mind, your body.

Will you sing a hymn now

With your eyes closed?

Awaiting the Union

As you lie burning

in a faraway land,

away from the people

you once knew,

revelation dawns on

you like a white light

that you and your

supreme being are yet

to unite. The worldly

pangs apart, you aspire

for the union.

Alone you contemplate

of the supreme soul

and creation flows.

The Journey

The mother of all creation

handholds you and guides

you through your journey within.

As you sit still and contemplate

you race through the creation,

crimson red, beyond the

azure sky. The voids rush

at you but you are not shaken

as you know you have

to travel beyond it,

your faith the energy to

move on. Beyond the

creation, beyond the void

Pranab Ghosh   -   Soul Searching
and other poems

your journey ends and

you are engulfed by

the eternal light.

You are illuminated.

Lord's Abode

In the diffused light

of the morning,

when the workmen

go to the mill,

I see you following

them in shabby dress,

much like what they

have worn. You reside

in the hutments

they stay in.

In their work you

come alive and through

their work they pay

you obeisance

unknowingly though.

When did you leave

the temple to stay

in their hutments

I know not, as I look

for you in vain

in your official abode

amidst burning incense

sticks and flowers.

To you I dedicate

my words, my work.

On a Rainy Evening

The first shower has

kissed the dusty roads.

As you walk down the

muddied streets

you see the rain-bathed

trees greener than before.

The city is at peace

with the scorching

summer sun going

beneath the gray clouds.

In the pale light

Of the evening you see

Pranab Ghosh   -   Soul Searching
       and other poems

the lone soldier with

his killing machine

slung by his shoulder

walk by. You fail to

Understand his presence.

In the pale evening light

as you remember your love

you fail to understand

why wars are waged,

why man kills man.

In the pale light of the evening

you want to forget and forgive.

Tulips in the Graveyard

Whispering willows speak

to the night, buried in

the grave.

Land where

once tulips grew lie

barren.

Chirp of

birds is silenced by

the sound of bullets.

Man dies fighting for

vain cause. They lie

murdered in their attempts

to become martyrs.

Pranab Ghosh   -   Soul Searching
and other poems

Sighs of widows and

bereaved mothers make

the trees sway at night.

Nocturnal animals lurk

as man kills man in

the name of jihad.

Dead bodies rot in

a world turned into hell

by their jest to adorn

the heaven.

The cause of God is best served

by erasing tears from

the eyes of the suffering

mankind. Instead they

make man suffer.

Agonies apart let the

world unite in peace.

Let tulips cover the

graveyard. Let us dig

no new grave to bury

the young.

Let nations

join hands to erase poverty

and humiliation that

man suffers from the

hand of man.

Let there

be a world where no

soldiers roam to

keep peace.

Let children

play in the streets that

turn into battle grounds

where baton-wielding

policemen thrash stone

pelting protestors. Let

clashes be a thing of

the past.

Let civilization rise

from the ashes and

proclaim to the world

that God had created the

universe and Man has

made the world.

Bathing in memories

Green sways in thin air, drenched in rain.

A lone bird flies across the sky.

Memories take wings, and float

In the rain-soaked morning sky,

Waiting for the sun to brighten them up.

Grief rises from the depths of the soul,

Making the air misty.

You look at the grey sky with blurred eyes.

Faces come and go.

They play hide and seek with the cloud.

Pranab Ghosh   -   Soul Searching
and other poems

Rain moistens them, and like wet birds

They jerk the water off them.

Remembrances float in the air,

Get linked to one another;

Some happy, some sad;

Some tell a tale of a union,

Some talk of severance,

As drops of rain fall on your cheeks,

Your hand, chest and back.

Rain-soaked,

You bathe in your memories.

The Tank

The water trembles

holding the reflection

of the morning sun.

A street urchin throws

a stone at the sun,

the ripples reach

the shore.

There is a woman washing

clothes on the bank.

She bathes there everyday

sharing space with the sun.

Pranab Ghosh   -   Soul Searching
and other poems

In the evening the moon

replaces the sun and

the silver water stands

still reflecting the voices

of the local belles who

gather on the bank

bathing in the cool breeze.

Their laughter creates

ripples in the water

that dissolves in

the middle.

The tank lies still

through the night

listening to the crickets

and reflecting the

*Pranab Ghosh   -   Soul Searching
             and other poems*

flying bats silhouetted

against the sinking moon.

The local belles then

dream of their lovers.

Water whispers in their ears.

Super consciousness

He waits for you patiently.

He knows you will return.

The light within you

is your guide. The flight

path is chalked. You

handhold your guru,

and embark on the

mysterious journey one

day. You travel through the

space, the void and

the creation and beyond.

You find Him waiting for

you. You are united

with Him. Now you

are super conscious.

The self matters no more.

Your birth is no longer

an enigma, for you have

travelled the distance,

between creation and void

and have met the

Supreme Soul beyond

the universe of senses.

Life's come a full circle

now and you are eager

to create and recreate.

His Master's Creation

In front of your majestic presence

words tend to falter,

as we stand mesmerized

admiring your installation.

The gravelled ground

so different from the

red soil that adorn

the place is home to

the tallest beauties

of the earth, proudly

saluting the sun.

The deep gorges

with scars created

by water are like

wrinkles on the skin

of an old beauty, who

has transcended time

and have become

immortal. In front

of that timeless beauty

we stand with heads

bowed to you

in loving reverence.

We salute your creation

and poetry takes

shape deep within us.

We sing to your creation.

Revolution

Perspiration trickles down

your temple, moistens your

eyelids and threatens to

enter your eyes.

You mop your face on

the shirt sleeve, anchal of

your saree, your dupatta;

you are too excited

to use your handkerchief

as you raise your voice

against oppression and tyranny.

You want to fight, to cry for

those who have suffered.

*Pranab Ghosh   -   Soul Searching
and other poems*

You want to raise your fist

in a unique display of solidarity

You want to revolt.

Meditation

As you sit erect,

your mind touching

your soul

and wait for the light

to shepherd you

beyond the void,

you touch your

life within.

The mind flies,

beyond the horizon,

beyond the void,

beyond the azure creation

*Pranab Ghosh   -   Soul Searching
              and other poems*

beyond the crimson red

turbulence,

beyond everything

and embrace the

eternal light.

Brightness all around

blinds you.

You sit blessed…

You meditate.

March

The sun is burning the earth;

water taps run dry at noon;

the pitch on the road melts

making your slipper stick

to it, as you file past

houses, malls, restaurants

and shops, carrying flags

and posters, raising slogan

against the oppressor,

the ruling combine that has

usurped men and women

of the right to protest.

You walk in a long queue

Pranab Ghosh - Soul Searching
and other poems

along one side of the road

so as not to disrupt traffic.

You sweat, your mouth runs dry,

but you froth to raise

your voice for your rights.

You walk with others

to bring change and justice.

You are part of a

procession, a rally

as you march ahead.

Mantra

Where would chant of mantras

take us to?

Cravings die inside us

as desire burns like wild fire

devouring our very dream.

We rush back to God

as if to implore Him

to step in and rescue us

from the catastrophe.

The chant saves our soul

as we gather strength

to live on.

Chant the hymn…

Chant the prayer…

Till you die

to live!

Emergency

In this startled time

we breathe together,

we are brethren.

In this startled time

we live together,

we are family.

In this startled time

we speak together,

we are association.

In this startled time

Pranab Ghosh   -   Soul Searching
*   and other poems*

we hold hands and

walk the street

like lovers from

another world.

In this startled time,

we struggle to live

as if it were a period

after revolution.

In this startled time,

life, relations and love

are all kept in

suspended animation.

To continue living

is an emergency.

Desire

Desire is like a symphony in a void.

Desire is like a distant dream

you seldom remember when

you wake up.

Desire is like the thirst

you feel after you

wake up dead in the night.

Desire is like the morning

breeze that takes you

back to your childhood.

Desire is like a forgotten melody

you hum in your sleep.

Desire is like forbidden love

*Pranab Ghosh - Soul Searching
and other poems*

you taste only in dream.

Is desire a dream?

What's the harm then

to dream of you?

Waiting for the Sun

The overcast sky

like your pale face

stares at the morning.

Dreams and desire

mingle in the diffused

light of the day.

Mired in melancholy

you stand at a

distance trying to

bathe in the morning

breeze. Images cross

your mind. You

feel shaken by the

dark thoughts that

resemble the gray

clouds. You wait

for the sun to

brighten up your

soul and fill

the blue sky

with light, white

and pure. You

wait for the purity

of the morning to

return and I

embrace you to

whisper in your ears.

Betrayed

As I lay in your arms

thinking of the forgotten

dreams and the times

of joy we walked through

together not so long

ago, you think of

your lover. Betrayed,

I lie frigid as you

caress me in unmindful

desire. I feel like

throwing up, as images

of your mistress and

you devouring each

other cross my mind.

Tears moisten my

cheeks as you sink

inside me in false

gesture of love that

rots in your gut

and burns my flesh.

I want to pluck

you from the depths

of my body and

throw you in a

litter bin. I want to

shred you into pieces.

Trading of the Soul

The sleepless night

has been long.

He tossed on the

bed, tormented by

desire. She lay

asleep by his side

unaware of the rot

he was experiencing.

As night became darker

he became overpowered

by perverse longing.

His flesh burned.

*Pranab Ghosh   -   Soul Searching
and other poems*

His soul had left

him long ago when

he exchanged it

for power. Tonight

he lay powerless

wanting to die by

the side of the lady

he once loved.

His deepest secret fears

engulfed him. He

thought of a day

when he was stripped

of all worldly belongings.

His heart convulsed.

He lay motionless

enduring the pain.

The night he traded

his soul in company

of his lover, he remembered

his love for once.

But he brushed her

images aside. Tonight

writhing in pain, his

bowels twisting, he

wants to turn the clock.

But that is not to be.

Mefisto came and

went that night, and he

became a lump of flesh,

*Pranab Ghosh   -   Soul Searching
    and other poems*

unaware of the decay

he had set within him.

He has lost his vigour.

He can no longer satisfy

the siren who accompanied

him that night when

he lost the protection

of the Lord. Tonight

satan will also desert him.

He pines for the lost purity

of his soul, desiring for

the dark night to end.

His days are also dark,

but at least he could

stare at the sun-filled sky

forgetting the cry

of his lost soul.

Nights are unbearable, with

his tormented soul

craving to be freed

from the slavery of a

heartless master, as

he suffers night after night

lying by the side

of the lady who is

unaware of the trade.

Souls are traded in

the darkest of nights

and he has nothing

Pranab Ghosh - Soul Searching
and other poems

to offer now as he

waits for his flesh

to perish and die.

Union Within

Alone I contemplated

of the night you were

with me. Eternal light

invaded me as you

embraced me. I remembered

of a celestial union

light years away.

Ours is a different

union where two

entities become one.

Deep inside me I

felt your presence.

Loneliness disappeared.

New Poetry

Red Krishnachuda lie

scattered by the road side.

She walks like a queen down

the road; her bare back

reflecting the morning sun.

The world was devastated

last night. Fierce wind

had tossed trees aside.

Hutments were razed

to the ground. Her home

withstood the fury.

Pranab Ghosh - *Soul Searching*
and other poems

She is going to fetch water

from the lost river

fed by the last night's rain.

She walks alone with

pitcher on her head.

Her gait has a music,

the earthen flute

played by the wind.

The melody has engulfed

my soul giving rise

to new poetry.

Mother

She sits still in front

of the television, staring

blankly at the screen.

Sound and light and

images dance around

her; she can barely

figure out what is

happening, as her mind

travels through the

open window out into

the darkness where her

husband has disappeared.

*Pranab Ghosh - Soul Searching
and other poems*

Nights bring back

memories of her youth,

when her son was

young and husband

worked in the factory.

Now, she can barely

move, her activities

beyond her control.

She escapes into

the television screen

sharing space with

unfamiliar faces,

crying and smiling, without

registering anything. Night

after night after night. She

can no longer bear the escape.

She wanders in the darkness

outside, where she finally

wants to disappear.

Old Boys' Club

Boyish faces float in

from oblivion. Dusty

memories fail to keep

company. The smile, the

giggle, the hurrah that

time has erased will

not come alive once again;

only the memories of

a forgotten past will

liven the stay.

Weather-worn, war-weary

wrinkles beside the eyes

*Pranab Ghosh - Soul Searching
and other poems*

and noses will brighten

up and be soothed for

a moment, as laughter

of yesteryears will

raise a ripple in the

pond and in it

will float old boys'

faces by the side

of waterlillies and

lotuses.

Birds may or

may not chirp; the

crimson red evening

sky will bend its neck

to look at the old boys' club.

*Pranab Ghosh   -   Soul Searching
and other poems*

And in the evening light

we will embrace

our memories.

Reunion

Mind that loves can

inflict pain. Vision

stands paralysed

as passion floats

in the thin night air

embracing memories.

It was perhaps another

era that you made

love to me. I think

it was only yesterday.

Today dull pain numbs my

thought process and

Pranab Ghosh   -   Soul Searching
and other poems

I sit askance wondering

at what might have

peeved you. I endure

the pain in memory

of yesterday.

Night lies naked in

front of my eyes.

Desire swirls in

the vein as blood

rush to the heart

in anticipation. To

endure pain is perhaps

testimony to love.

Pain apart, we unite again.

Pranab Ghosh - Soul Searching and other poems

Dead Desire

Desire rises from the

depths of the naval;

The snake within

recoils; life shudders

as the parted lips

show a new earning

that skimmed the elixir

of life from the depths

of the ocean with the

eternal reptile recoiling

from the tug, bleeding

all over, its venom

exhausted.

*Pranab Ghosh   -   Soul Searching
and other poems*

Volcano erupted. Love

lay dead. Frigid

body shook from

 the touch. Pent-up love

uncoiled and the

yearning dissolved in

the azure sea.

Sun gleamed above

the head. Hungry

souls danced in joy

for having escaped the

all-encompassing flow

of the molten death.

They now float on the

ocean with sun sharing

with them the

testimony of life.

Desire lives, as pouts

morph into smile of

separated lovers reuniting

in life beyond death.

The snake lay dead

at the bed of the ocean.

Demonetised Winter

The time that never was

stands in front of you

and questions your very

existence; your rights

usurped, you are denied

a chance even to explain.

It is winter. But it is

nothing like what winter

used to be. You stand

in the sun and sweat.

The question that keeps

turning in your head makes

*Pranab Ghosh - Soul Searching
and other poems*

you sweat more than the

December sun.

Your existence no longer

matters to them you

thought would care.

The semblance of

care that made you

stand still in front

of the time that never was

dissapears and you look

around to find unknown

faces going through the same

existential agony you thought

they would never recognise.

*Pranab Ghosh   -   Soul Searching
and other poems*

Power passes by, siren

hooting. Those in the

convoy look at you.

Was there pity in their

eyes for you and those

rotting under the sun?

Or was there a sense of

victory reflected in

those eyes that seem

to have by-passed the

time that never was?

The question turns in

your head. You look for answers.

Images crop up. Dead man

lying by the footpath,

*Pranab Ghosh - Soul Searching
and other poems*

his search for money

no longer a reality.

The agony continues for

others who will have to

live. It is for them the

time that will always be…

Blessed Dead

Life has become static.

Like living dead bodies

we move.

We have no direction.

Life's become like an

abandoned construction work

mired in litigation.

But there is hectic pace.

Dead bodies rush

to occupy space

in offices, hospitals, malls and
theatres.

*Pranab Ghosh - Soul Searching
and other poems*

Blessed are the dead,

Who do not move.

Remembering a Friend

I do not remember

When I last saw him.

I do not remember

the jokes we shared,

the time we spent together,

the opinions we exchanged.

I do not remember when

We became men.

I do not remember

When he got married,

When his first child was born,

When he got divorced.

*Pranab Ghosh - Soul Searching
and other poems*

I do not remember

whether I knew him at all.

Swearing by the eyes

Her eyes reflected

the agony of the earth.

In their depths was hidden

the pain of birth and death.

Her eyes reflected

the solitude of her mind.

The loneliness that you suffer from when

in a crowd.

Her eyes reflected

deep desire, the

Pranab Ghosh   -   Soul Searching
and other poems

pangs of unfulfilled

wishes, of boredom

of the dreary

daily existence that

you want to run away from.

Her eyes had invitation

writ large on it.

An invitation to overcome

the depths of sorrow

and traverse the

world beyond grief

to a moment's fulfilment

in mysterious secrecy.

Her eyes held love,

lust, pain and grief.

Her eyes reflected

her soul waiting

to be freed from the sufferings of the body.

She wanted me to

journey with her

to the forbidden land

with her eyes

swearing to maintaining

the secrecy.

Inaction

Revolution is red

so is what is underneath;

your breasts are held

in absolute awe

as you move down the stairs

leaving your lemonade

for him to stir.

A smoke apart I cross you;

revolution red lingerie

inviting action,

I fail to act

as poetry sits quietly

in front of a cup of coffee,

*Pranab Ghosh   -   Soul Searching
and other poems*

breast thrust forward

hands fiddling in the air.

I give it a passing tribute,

but fail to act.

The poetess was sitting close by,

all attention to the unwritten verse.

She was expecting lines to arrive,

but I failed to act.

"Inaction" was the word

written on the wall.

Hint of a Smile

There was a hint of smile

on her lips, years ago.

Looking back, we travelled

in time.

The unwritten invitation

had all along been there.

But we couldn't live

between the sheets

to transcend time

and nights.

I saw her yesterday

amidst fleeting street lights.

Was there still that

*Pranab Ghosh - Soul Searching
and other poems*

hint of smile?

Where Were You?

I wanted to meditate

but went to sleep.

Faces and dreams

invaded me.

Were you there?

Deep inside me

I felt you move.

My soul stirred.

Waiting for the New Leaf

A leaf is turned

Life stares at you…

A blank look, from

A blank space…

You do not know

Where to go … what

Is in store as you

Look back to find

An answer.

***Pranab Ghosh - Soul Searching
and other poems***

A leaf is turned and

There are images

Standing side by side…

Letters piling up to

Form sentences that

You cannot read…

Nor do you know what

The images are. You

Try to find meaning…

Meaning that will bring

Sense back and destroy

The uncertain times

you are in.

Pranab Ghosh   -   Soul Searching
and other poems

A leaf is turned and

You find yourself standing

In front of a void that

You want to fill…

Memories come and go…

New Year arrives with

No new destiny, as you

Languish from the bite

Of a jobless time, looking

Ahead to a future that

Is all gloom with

No visible respite!

Pranab Ghosh   -   Soul Searching
and other poems

A leaf is turned;

There is cash crunch

In the market suffering

From demonetization of

High value currencies.

Till the other day you

Had the surety of a

Month-end pay cheque

Now it is gone as if

A dream has come

To an end, but the

Night ahead is long.

Pranab Ghosh   -   Soul Searching
      and other poems

You try to sleep to

Catch another dream,

But you toss and turn.

Sweat trickles down

Your forehead; what

If it is winter?

A leaf is turned,

And in front of you

Stand eager expectant

Faces that depend

On you. You had brought

Smile on those before…

Pranab Ghosh   -   Soul Searching
and other poems

You know not whether there

Would be smile tomorrow

As you wait for another leaf

To turn that will bring new

Light, new meaning and

Smile back to you and

Those dependent on you.

You wait for the New Leaf!

*Pranab Ghosh   -   Soul Searching
and other poems*

Better Dead

Smoke spirals out of the

Two fingers…

The cigarette burns.

You puff at it … one

Two… three… four…

Five… there is no break;

As you exhale a thin

Layer forms and

Slowly withers into the

Night outside. It's one o'clock.

Pranab Ghosh   -   Soul Searching
and other poems

The smoke disappears into

The air that embraces

A sky without a single

Star… without any light

That nights otherwise have.

You look at it for direction.

Is there cloud up there?

In the evening the sky was

Clear blue. Did you

Spot the moon then?

Why has darkness, darker

Pranab Ghosh - Soul Searching
　and other poems

Than the night has descended

On earth? Why has the

Stars gone into a hiding? Why

Are there no street lights

To illuminate the horizon?

Far away beyond the horizon

Is there a hint of light?

The darkness perhaps is

Symbolic of the time

That we are in; of the

Time that has engulfed

Us, where people stand

Pranab Ghosh   -   Soul Searching
      and other poems

In long queues to take

Out their money

From the banks and ATMs. A few

Of them do not return home

With money so desperately

Needed by their loved ones!

They die while standing in queue!

People file pass the dead;

They are more anxious to lay

their hands on their money

than helping the dying.

Could the dead not have lived

Pranab Ghosh   -   Soul Searching
and other poems

If help was at hand!

The dark night outside has no

answer;

As you stare at the darkness

outside,

You perhaps are aware that

You are alive but, you

Are too scared to

Acknowledge it. Perhaps

You were better off dead,

With no queues to stand in,

No loans to repay, no family

To feed and no urge to

*Pranab Ghosh - Soul Searching
and other poems*

Earn a living. Perhaps you

Were better dead!

Ode to Manhood

He is a high school boy,

Stays in apartment block 'o'

Bang opposite his block oh toy!

Lives a model of size 'zero'.

She comes back home at 8 o'clock
every evening

And removes the curtains of her
windows with great yearning!

With her mind's eye, she spots

Pranab Ghosh   -   Soul Searching
and other poems

The boy, who from his darkened room with camera shots

The beauty down to her bare essentials

And she contemplates of rescuing from him all her testimonials!

The high school boy has gone crazy,

Because every evening she sends him into a tizzy

With her pleasant undress

That puts the boy under extreme duress!

Enough of hide and seek

Thinks the boy and takes a decision sleek

To confront his object of passion,

When every morning she goes for her gym session.

That morning was out of the world

When the boy met the lady up there

*Pranab Ghosh   -   Soul Searching
and other poems*

Right in front of the apartment block

With her scarf hiding her lock.

The boy could not find his words

The lady helped him by unlocking her hair

'You are lovely,' blurts the boy,

Oh! Thinks the lady this is a nice toy.

The game begins in all earnest

Pranab Ghosh   -   Soul Searching
and other poems

With the boy giving his dream

Every morning a chase in real jest

And one Wednesday after the gym

They together had ice-cream.

This is heaven! This is bliss!

Thinks the boy

When next Wednesday she gives him a kiss.

But how long would last his joy?

The lady wanted the boy to be prudent

Because she found in her company he grows diffident.

The crush is all very fine

If it teaches the boy to toe her line.

She is a model aspiring

Would to become a model be the boy's yearning?

The boy has no answer

As he wants to be a photographer.

The model and the photographer
can work together

And be with each other ever after!

I am too old for you o boy!

To me you are just a nice toy!

Together we could be for sure

But your romantic dreams

Pranab Ghosh - Soul Searching and other poems

You will have to abjure

The boy gave it a thought

His passion for lens too great

For an alternative to be sought.

The crush comes to an end

With the lady getting a young man
to tend!

Workman's Hero

Pain in the lower back…

Pain in the neck…

Pain in the back of the head…

Pain in the mind gone numb!

They say you are becoming aware,

They say you are getting illuminated.

I say it's karma baby,

Not only of yours, but others' too

That's making you numb,

*Pranab Ghosh   -   Soul Searching
and other poems*

As evening sets in.

It's soul-transfer time baby.

The dusk will dawn on you.

It's time for some fun baby,

As you lay still,

Unable to move.

It's Lenon or it's Marx?

Tell me who you want to be?

I want to be a workman's hero

That's all I want to be!

By Pranab Ghosh

*Pranab Ghosh -   Soul Searching
and other poems*

Pranab Ghosh - Soul Searching and other poems

Afterword

Hope you have liked reading these assortments of varied cookies, poems of all hues. There were poems based on deep realization, the foundation of which had been great concentration bordering on meditation on the self, as also there were poems like Tulips in the Graveyard, which is basically an anti-war, anti-terrorism, anti-violence poem upholding the human spirit above everything else. There were also dark poems based on erosion of human values and men's craving for power, which in turn destroys man. There were also poems like Revolution and March juxtaposed with poems like Mantra.

Man's craving to stand up against all that is negative, all that is against human values – to stand up against oppression and injustice had been juxtaposed with man's eternal wish to take refuge in the Eternal, the

Divine. Side by side poems of great human values, there are lighter reads on love bordering on mischievous take on the fair sex.

Hope you have liked reading everything. And if I have annoyed you with my view point, I look forward to being forgiven. Over and above I look for love from you, my readers. Love me and my creation and share your feelings with your friends. Ask them to read Soul Searching as well. Hope I am not imposing myself on your good self.

Thank you!

*Pranab Ghosh   -   Soul Searching
and other poems*

Author's Bio

Pranab Ghosh is a journalist, writer, poet, translator and blogger. He writes a blog "Existential Problems".

He graduated from Scottish Church College, Kolkata, with Honours in English. He did his masters in Journalism from Calcutta University. He has also done a course in Creative English from British Council, New Delhi.

He has worked for such media houses as HT Media Ltd, Eenadu India etc. He has written for Slant News, an US news portal and such publications as The Statesman, Economic Times, Ei Samay. At present he writes for Business India.

Pranab Ghosh - Soul Searching and other poems

His poems and prose pieces have been published and accepted by Tuck Magazine, Transendent Zero Press, Scarlet Leaf Review, Literature Studio Review, Leaves of Ink, Hans India, Dissident Voice etc.

He has coauthored a book of poems, titled Air & Age. He has to his credit a translation of a book of Bengali short stories titled Shantiramer Cha, authored by Bitan Chakraborty. The title of the English translation is Bougainvillea and Other Stories.

He is married and lives in Kolkata with wife, daughter and mother.

*Pranab Ghosh   -   Soul Searching
and other poems*

Acknowledgements

The following poems first appeared in Tuck Magazine:

> *March, Mantra, Emergency, Desire, Super consciousness, His Master's Creation, Revolution, Meditation, Dead Desire, Demonetised winter.*

The following poems first appeared in Scarlet Leaf Review:

> *Soul Searching, Awaiting the Union, The Journey, Lord's Abode, On a Rainy Evening, Waiting for the Sun, Betrayed, Trading of the Soul, Union Within, New Poetry, Workman's Hero, Ode to*

Pranab Ghosh - Soul Searching and other poems

Manhood, Better Dead, Waiting for the New Leaf.

The following poem first appeared in Dissident Voice:

Tulips in the Graveyard.

The following poem first appeared in The Leaves of Ink:

The Tank.

The following poems first appeared in Literature Studio Review:

Hint of a smile, Where were you?

The following poem first appeared in Hans India:

Bathing in memories.

*Pranab Ghosh - Soul Searching
and other poems*

Pranab Ghosh - Soul Searching and other poems

Table of Contents

Soul Searching 6

Awaiting the Union 8

The Journey 10

Lord's Abode 12

On a Rainy Evening 14

Tulips in the Graveyard 16

Bathing in memories 20

The Tank 22

Super consciousness 25

His Master's Creation 27

Revolution 29

Meditation 31

March 33

Mantra 35

Emergency 37

Desire 40

Waiting for the Sun 42

*Pranab Ghosh   -   Soul Searching
and other poems*

Betrayed 44

Trading of the Soul 46

Union Within 52

New Poetry 53

Mother 55

Old Boys' Club 58

Reunion 61

Dead Desire 63

Demonetised Winter 66

Blessed Dead 70

Remembering a Friend 72

Swearing by the eyes 74

Inaction 77

Hint of a Smile 79

Where Were You? 81

Waiting for the New Leaf 82

Better Dead 88

Ode to Manhood 94

Workman's Hero 102

*Pranab Ghosh   -   Soul Searching
and other poems*

Afterword 105

Author's Bio 108

Acknowledgements 111

Pranab Ghosh - Soul Searching and other poems

Pranab Ghosh's Soul Searching and Other Poems is a collection of several verses with varied flavor and source. While Ghosh, as I found him a loner, is engaged in exploring 'self,' his other poems are essentially derived from the material world. A must read book, especially whoever appreciates philosophy in verses.

Kiriti Sengupta

www.kiritisengupta.com

*Pranab Ghosh   -   Soul Searching
and other poems*

www.ingramcontent.com/pod-product-compliance
Lightning Source LLC
Chambersburg PA
CBHW070150080526
44586CB00015B/1921